D1606775

CARS

Consultant
Walter L. Metzelfeld
Automotive Instructor
Milwaukee Area Technical College

Copyright © 1981, Raintree Publishers Inc.

Library of Congress Number: 80-17876

2 3 4 5 6 7 8 9 0 84 83 82

Printed and bound in the United States of America.

Library of Congress Cataloging in Publication Data

Clark, James I.
  Cars.

  (A Look inside)
  Includes index.
  SUMMARY: An overview of the braking and electrical
systems, engine, and transmission of cars and an
examination of unusual models and possible alternative
energy sources for cars.
  1. Automobiles — Juvenile literature.
[1. Automobiles] I. Dyess, John. II. Bailey, John
Michael, 1946- III. Title. IV. Series: Look
inside.
TL147.C5   629.2   80-17876
ISBN 0-8172-1405-4 (lib. bdg.)

CARS

By James Clark

Illustrated by John Bailey/Bercker Studios Ltd
 and John Dyess
Cover illustration by Mark Mille

CONTENTS

RAINTREE PUBLISHERS
Milwaukee • Toronto • Melbourne • London

UNDER THE HOOD

There are all kinds of cars. Some are as small as go-carts, others are as large as small airplanes. Some cars have two doors, others four. A few even have six doors. Some have two seats, some only one.

Most cars use gasoline as their fuel. But some run on diesel fuel. Others may soon be running on electricity.

We're going to talk mostly about just one kind of car. The engine is in the front. Power goes from the engine to the rear wheels. The car runs on gasoline.

But wait. That's not quite all. After we talk about what makes a car that uses gasoline go, we'll talk about some different kinds of cars, and also a little about different kinds of engines.

To some people, a car is a thing of beauty. To others, it's just a way to get around. And to many people in both groups, a car is mainly four wheels, seats, and a steering wheel.

What makes a car go? That's simple.

You slide into the driver's seat. You close the door and fasten your safety belt. Then you place a key in a little slot and turn it. The engine starts and away you go. That's all.

That's not all, of course. There is much more to making a car go than that.

It all comes down to energy. Heat or electrical energy changes into mechanical energy to make the car move. But there are many steps along the way.

First of all, what really makes the engine start? Part of the answer is electricity.

The electricity to start the engine comes first from the battery. This is a black box found near the engine, under the hood in front. The battery holds plates made of lead. It also contains a

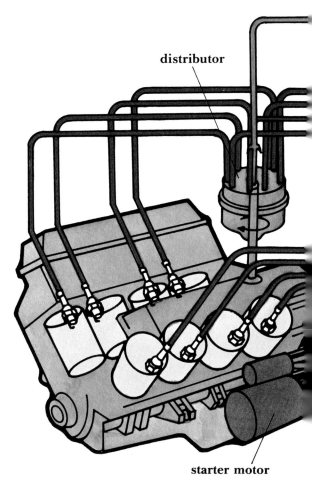

distributor

starter motor

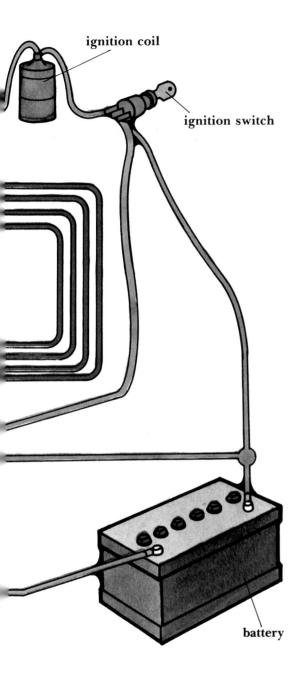

ignition coil

ignition switch

battery

mixture of acid and water. The plates and the mixture act together to make electricity in the battery.

The slot in which you place the key is called the ignition. "To ignite" means to light or to start. When you turn the key, the ignition sends an electrical signal to the battery to send out electricity.

You hear a whirring sound. This means that the battery has sent electricity to the starter motor, near the engine. The motor makes the sound. And it sends power to the crankshaft to make it turn. The crankshaft is found near the bottom of the engine. It is a long, crooked piece of metal, one with "humps" on it. Once the engine is started, the crankshaft can send power to the rear wheels to make them turn. But there are a few steps in between.

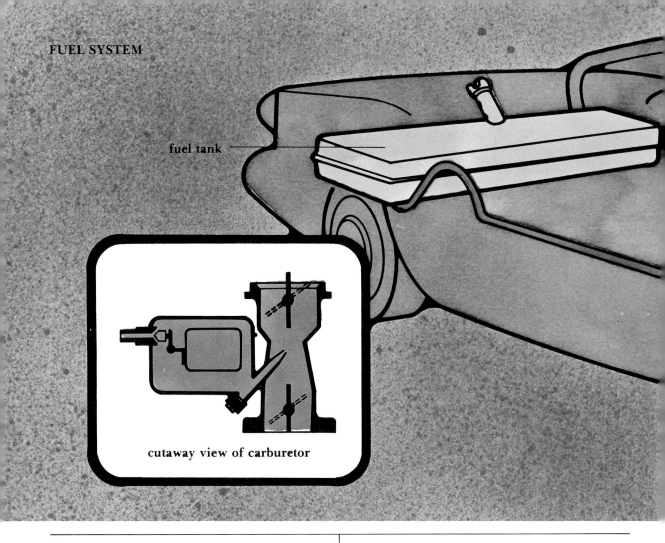

fuel tank

cutaway view of carburetor

Electricity from the battery is one part of what makes an engine start. The other part is gasoline and air.

A car carries gasoline in a tank. On most cars, the tank is found in the rear, under the trunk.

From the tank a small tube runs to a pump, called the fuel pump, on the engine. When the starter motor turns the crankshaft, the crankshaft starts the fuel pump. It sucks gasoline from the tank in much the same way that you suck a drink through a straw.

Now as we know, gasoline can explode. But first it must be mixed with air. A gas called

air filter

oxygen in the air helps make gasoline explode. Hot gases from the exploding gasoline are what give the engine power.

The fuel pump sends gasoline to the carburetor, which is basically a metal device on top of the engine. A large, round object called the air filter covers the carburetor.

Air from the outside is drawn through the filter. There it is cleaned and sent into the carburetor. The carburetor then shoots the air into a tube. At the same time, the carburetor acts like a squirt gun. It measures small drops of gasoline into the tube. There the air and the gasoline mix.

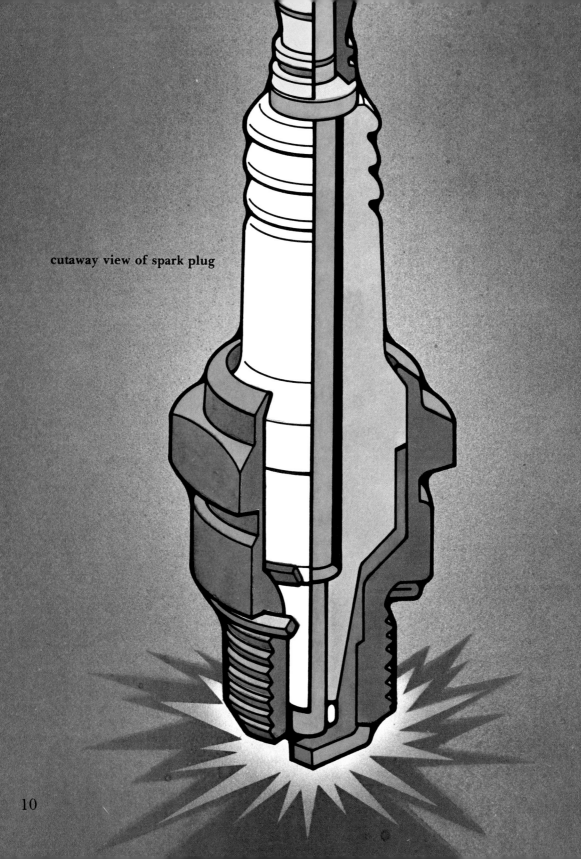

cutaway view of spark plug

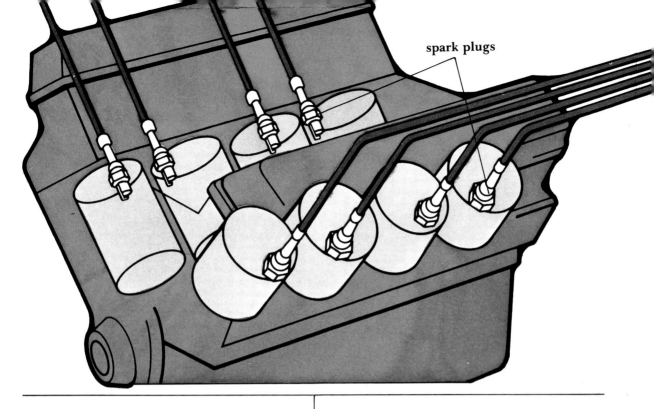

spark plugs

This alone is not enough to make the gasoline explode, though. There must also be some kind of heat. This heat comes from spark plugs.

You will find spark plugs near the top or sides of the engine. They stick out like small poles.

Spark plugs have wires at the top. These wires connect spark plugs to a part called the distributor. As you turn the ignition key, the battery sends electricity to the distributor. It does this at the same time it sends power to the starter motor.

The distributor passes the power to the spark plugs.

At the bottom of a spark plug are two small pieces of metal. They do not quite touch. Electricity from the distributor passes down one side of the plug. At the bottom, the electricity leaps from one piece of metal to the other. This causes a spark. The spark is the heat that "fires" the mixture of gasoline and air. It makes the mixture burn very fast. You could call it a controlled explosion!

A spark plug fits into the top of a cylinder. It is in the cylinder that the explosion takes place.

Cylinders are long, rounded tubes in a block of metal, which is the main part of the engine. An engine might have four, six, or eight cylinders. The larger the engine the more power it will have. Each cylinder has its own spark plug.

At the top of each cylinder there are two valves. A valve is like a lid. It opens and closes to let something in and out. One of the valves opens to let air and gasoline into the cylinder. Then it closes. This is called the intake valve. We'll get to the other valve in a moment.

Besides valves and a spark plug, each cylinder has a piston. A piston looks like a tin can. It fits inside the cylinder like an arm into a sleeve. The bottom of each piston is joined to the crankshaft by pieces of metal called connecting rods.

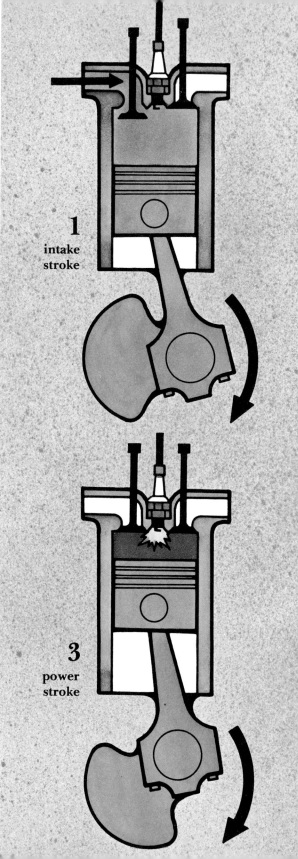

1
intake
stroke

3
power
stroke

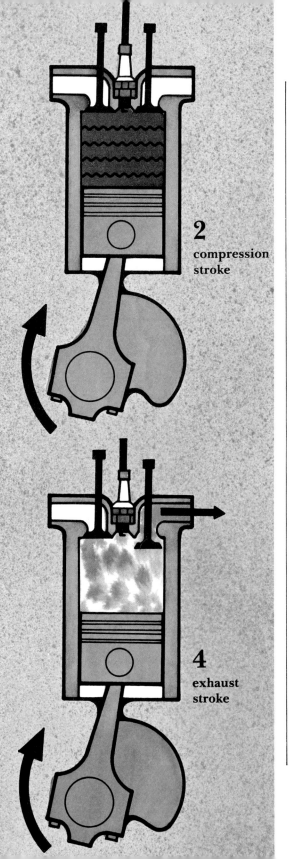

2
compression
stroke

4
exhaust
stroke

As the starter motor turns the crankshaft, it moves the pistons upward and downward. The carburetor shoots a mixture of gasoline and air through the intake valve into a cylinder where the piston is going down. The valve closes. The piston is near the top of the cylinder now. The spark jumps the gap on the spark plug and the mixture explodes. The burning gas expands, driving the piston down. This makes the crankshaft turn without the help of the starter motor.

We've looked at two parts of our answer to what makes an engine start — electricity, and gasoline and air. Now let's suppose we have a car with eight cylinders and put the whole picture together. A number of things happen at almost the same time. But we'll take them one by one.

First, you return to the ignition.

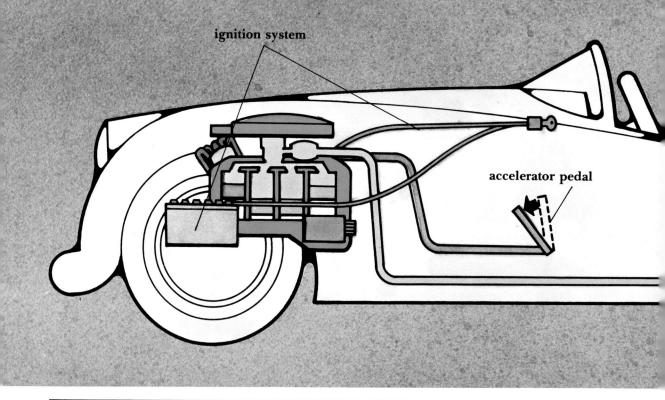

ignition system

accelerator pedal

You turn the key. This signals the battery to send power to the starter motor and to the distributor. The crankshaft begins to turn. The fuel pump sends gasoline to the carburetor. At the same time, you press your foot against a pedal on the floor. This is called the accelerator pedal. It opens a valve in the carburetor to let gasoline and air in. The carburetor mixes the air and gasoline.

Remember, the car we're talking about has eight cylinders with eight pistons. The crank-shaft is pulling some of the pistons down and pushing some of them up. The crooked shape of the crankshaft makes the pistons move in different directions.

Imagine eight people in a row doing knee bends. Up and down, up and down. This is how the pistons move.

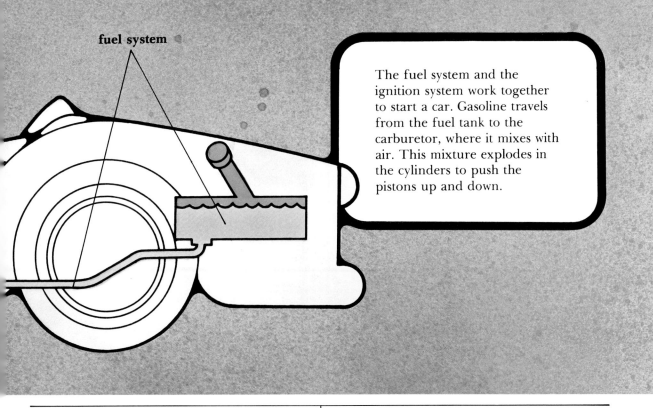

fuel system

The fuel system and the ignition system work together to start a car. Gasoline travels from the fuel tank to the carburetor, where it mixes with air. This mixture explodes in the cylinders to push the pistons up and down.

Now the carburetor shoots air and gasoline through the intake valve of one cylinder in which the piston is moving down. The valve closes. The piston coming up presses hard against the mixture. The spark plug fires. The mixture explodes. Down the piston goes. It moves the crankshaft and starts back up.

As this happens, another piston is near the top. The intake valve has opened and closed. A mixture is waiting. This piston also presses hard against the mixture. Another spark. Another explosion. The piston moves downward with great force. Then back up it comes.

Explosions come one right after another now — pow, pow, pow! But you don't hear them as explosions. They are too close together for that. Instead, you hear a purring noise from the engine. It is running smoothly.

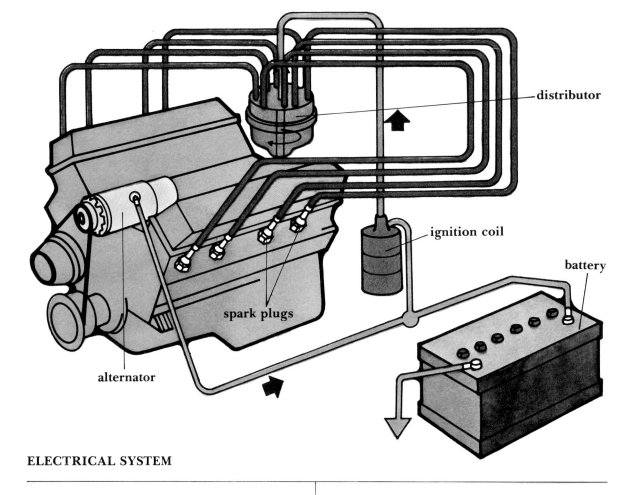

distributor

ignition coil

battery

spark plugs

alternator

ELECTRICAL SYSTEM

Moving up and down, the pistons keep the crankshaft turning. The starter motor is no longer needed. The battery is no longer needed either. The running engine makes electricity itself. It does so in a motor called the alternator. The alternator instead of the battery now sends power to the distributor. And the distributor sends that electricity to each spark plug in turn.

The alternator also sends electricity to the battery. This replaces the power from the battery that was used to start the engine. The alternator "recharges" the battery. This keeps it strong and ready when it is needed to start the car again.

Not all the mixture of air and gasoline in the cylinders burns. Some of it is waste. This waste is called exhaust.

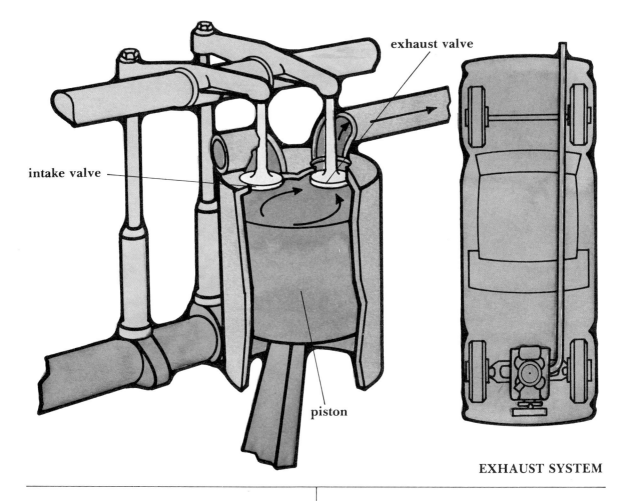

intake valve

exhaust valve

piston

EXHAUST SYSTEM

And this brings us to the other valve, besides the intake valve, in the cylinder. It is called the exhaust valve.

As we have seen, after moving down, each piston comes back up. As it does, the exhaust valve opens. The piston pushes the exhaust out of the cylinder. The exhaust valve closes. The waste passes through the exhaust pipe that runs along the bottom of the car. It leaves the car in the rear.

Exhaust from an engine is dirty. It pollutes the air. Engines now have devices to cut down on pollution. They clean much of the exhaust before it goes out through the pipe into the air.

UNDER THE FLOOR

The engine is running now, but our car is not going anywhere yet. Something else has to happen first. The engine's power must be carried to the car's rear wheels. (In a few cars the power goes to the front wheels.) This will make them turn and move the car. Let's look at this.

We said that the crankshaft sends power to the rear wheels. It does so by way of the output shaft.

The output shaft runs under the car floor to the rear. There it is connected to an axle. The axle is a long rod that connects the rear wheels. The axle makes those wheels turn.

Both the crankshaft and the output shaft turn in the same direction. The axle moves in another direction. So here we have a problem. How do we make the output shaft, which turns in one direction, turn the axle, which turns in another direction? Gears give us the answer.

A gear is a metal wheel with metal "teeth" around the outside. Gears are made so the teeth of one fit between the teeth of another.

Open your fingers wide. Place the fingers of one hand between those of the other. In other words, lace your fingers. This is how gear teeth come together.

There is a gear at the rear end of the output shaft. It moves in the same direction as the shaft. There is also a gear on the axle. This moves in the same direction as the axle. The teeth of the gears come together at right angles. As the output shaft moves in one direction, the gears cause the axle to turn in another direction.

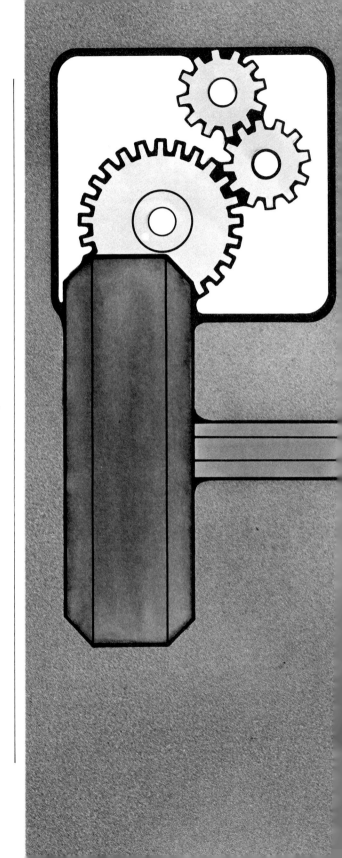

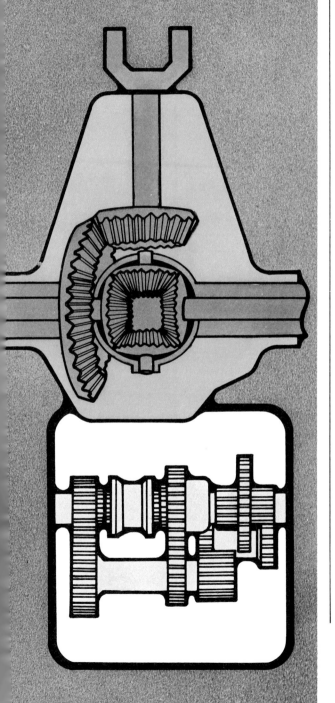

GEAR SYSTEMS

Before we can put the crankshaft and the output shaft together, though, we must look at some other gears. These are found in the transmission. The transmission is the system that carries the signals from the driver inside the car to the engine and the moving shafts.

The transmission is found behind the engine. It contains two shafts. One is the transmission shaft. The other is called the countershaft. Both shafts have gears on them. One gear on the countershaft connects to a gear on the output shaft.

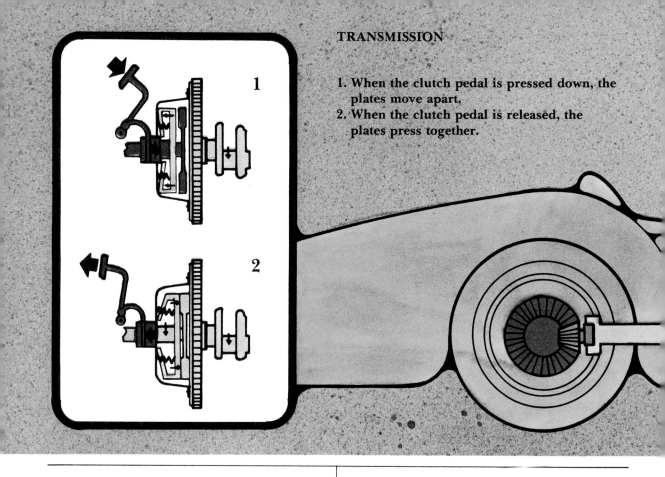

1. When the clutch pedal is pressed down, the plates move apart.
2. When the clutch pedal is released, the plates press together.

A clutch is also part of the transmission.

One kind of clutch is called the friction clutch. This is made of three round pieces of metal. One outside piece, called a plate, connects with the crankshaft. The other outside plate connects with the transmission shaft. The piece in the middle, called the disc, is rough on both sides.

When the two plates of the clutch come together against the disc, there is both friction and pressure. Pressure is a force that presses. Friction is a force that prevents things from moving easily.

To get an idea of pressure and friction, run your hand along a smooth surface. The top of a desk or a table will do. Your hand moves easily because the top is smooth. There is little friction. Now apply pressure.

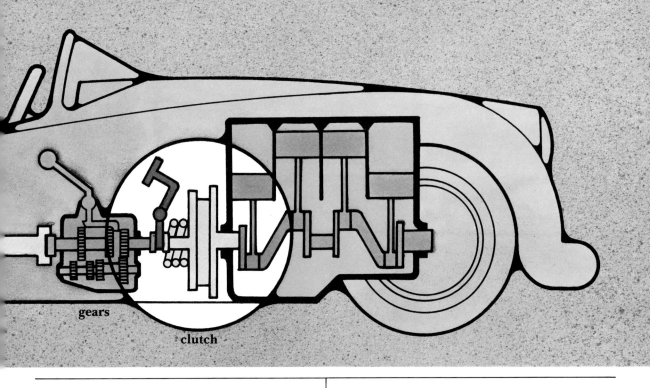

gears

clutch

Press down hard on the desk or tabletop. It still isn't very hard to move your hand, is it?

But now run your hand along a rough surface, like that of a rug. Here your hand doesn't move so easily. There is friction to hold it back. Now press down and try to move your hand. That's even harder. Both friction and pressure work against it.

In a friction clutch, the disc is like the rug. The two plates are like your hand. Pressure holds the three clutch parts together. Friction makes them turn together.

And as the parts of the clutch turn, gears on the crankshaft and the transmission shaft connect to one on the countershaft. That shaft sends power along the output shaft to the rear axle. The car moves.

But when we start our car, we don't want it to move right away. That would be dangerous. How do we prevent this?

We do so by making sure that no gear on the transmission shaft touches one on the countershaft until we want the car to move.

Sticking out of the floor of the car is a metal rod called a gearshift. By moving this to the "neutral" position, we can be sure that the gears are not touching one another, and that no power will flow to the output shaft and the rear axle. We know that the gears are in neutral when we can wriggle the gearshift freely.

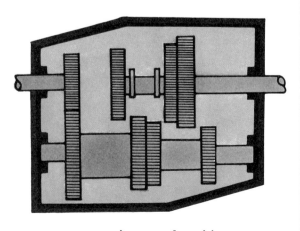

gears in neutral position

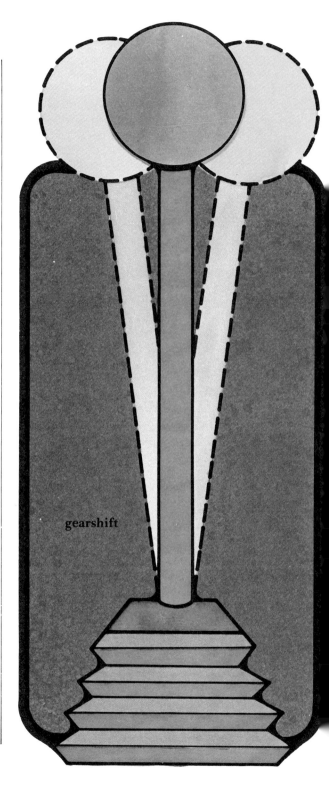

gearshift

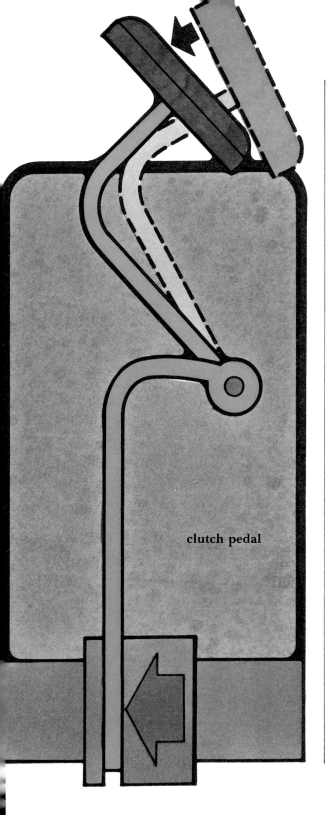

clutch pedal

Now our engine is warm and we want the car to move.

Under the driver's feet is found a pedal called the clutch pedal. Pressing this will move the clutch so its parts are not touching. As we press, we move the shift to "first gear," which is also called "low gear." When we do this, we cause the transmission shaft to move. It moves far enough to bring one of its gears together with a gear on the countershaft.

It takes a lot of power to get a car moving. The car is very heavy. There will be friction between the ground and the wheels.

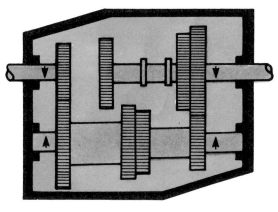

first gear

A small gear turning a large gear will produce much power. But it won't give much speed. So when we place the shift in first, we bring the teeth of a small gear on the transmission shaft between the teeth of a large gear on the countershaft.

The transmission shaft and the countershaft are now connected. We slowly raise our foot from the clutch pedal. The clutch closes. At the same time, we press the other foot gently on the accelerator. This feeds more gasoline and air into the carburetor. Power now flows from the transmission shaft to the countershaft to the output shaft to the rear axle to the wheels. Our car moves ahead, slowly.

We are now going about 15 to 20 miles (24 to 32 kilometers) an hour. The engine no longer has to work so hard. So we are ready to change into "second gear."

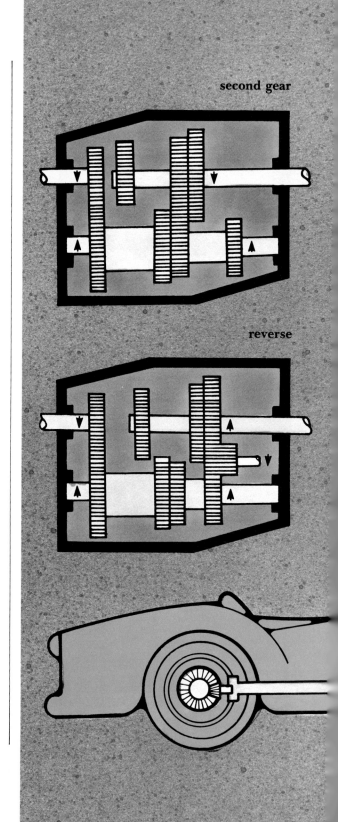

second gear

reverse

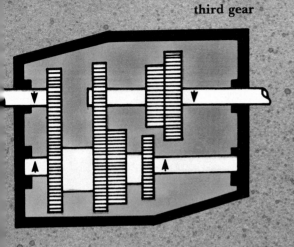

third gear

Notice that as we shift gears, different gears in the transmission are connected. In reverse, the direction of the gears changes.

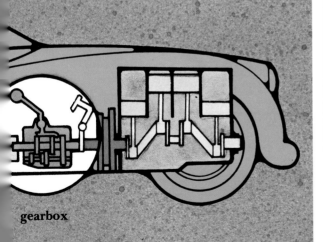

gearbox

First we let up on the accelerator. Then we again press the clutch pedal. This moves the gears apart while we shift to second gear. This bring a larger gear on the transmission shaft together with a smaller gear on the countershaft.

Slowly we let the clutch pedal out. The clutch parts come together to make the power connection again. Our car is moving faster now, and more easily.

As we reach 25 to 30 miles (40 to 48 kilometers) an hour, we're ready for one more gear change. We go through the same motions again and shift into "third gear." An even larger gear on the transmission shaft connects with yet a smaller one on the countershaft. This larger gear will not work as hard as the other two. Yet it will make the small gear turn fast. We are cruising along.

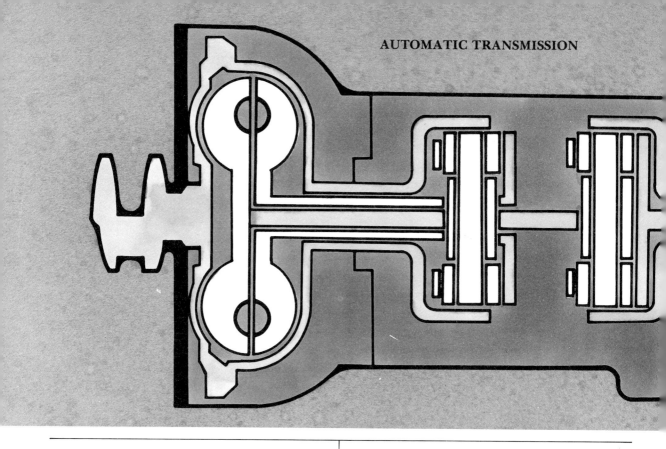

Sometimes there are one or two more gears, called "fourth" and "fifth." They are used when the car is moving very fast, as it does on a highway.

There is one gearshift position left. This is "reverse." Placing the gearshift in reverse brings two more gears on the transmission and the countershaft together. The countershaft and the output shaft turn in the opposite direction. The car moves backward.

Most cars today have automatic transmission. Here the idea of gears and the clutch is much the same. But this transmission has more gears and clutches.

A clutch in an automatic transmission is called a fluid clutch. It has two parts, which look like the parts of a doughnut cut down the middle. Inside both parts are curved blades. The blades face each other in a box filled with oil, which is a fluid.

fluid clutch

One set of blades connects with the crankshaft. As that turns, it spins the blades. Those blades throw oil against the blades in the other part, connected with the transmission shaft. The oil causes those blades to spin and turn that shaft.

A car with an automatic transmission has a gearshift too, but no clutch pedal. The gearshift has places for first and second gears. But usually the driver has only to put the shift in "drive." The transmission will then shift itself from first to second to third as the engine picks up speed.

Placing the shift in another position will put the transmission into reverse. Still another position is called "park." When the gearshift is in park, the car will not move. You cannot start the engine of many cars unless the shift is in park.

AROUND THE CAR

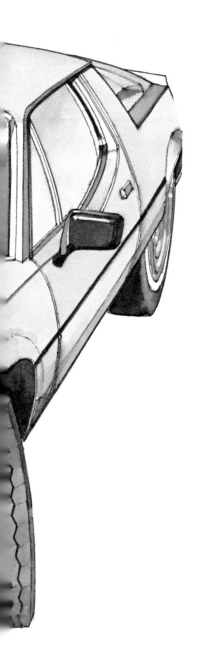

So far we've talked about a car's engine and the fuel system. We've seen how gasoline gets from the tank to the engine, and what happens to it there. We have also talked about what we call the power-train system. Using gasoline and air, the engine gives the car power. The power-train carries it to the rear axle.

These are only two of the systems a car has. Let's look at others. One is the steering system.

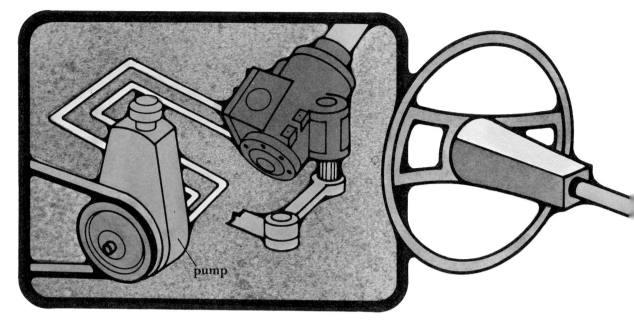

POWER STEERING

Everyone knows about the steering wheel. But that is only the part of the steering system you can see.

A metal rod joins the steering wheel to a box between the front wheels. Gears inside that box join the first rod to a second rod connected with the front wheels.

When you turn the steering wheel, the gears act together to carry power along the rod to move the wheels. This is called "manual" steering. The driver does much of the work.

Many cars have power steering. The idea here is much the same. But you use only a little muscle to steer the car. The driver gets help.

In power steering, there still are gears in a box between the wheels. The power to move them and the wheels comes from fluid that is pumped into the box. When you turn the steering wheel, you signal a small pump to set the fluid to work. Pressure from the fluid causes the gears, the rods, and the wheels to turn. Power steering makes driving easier.

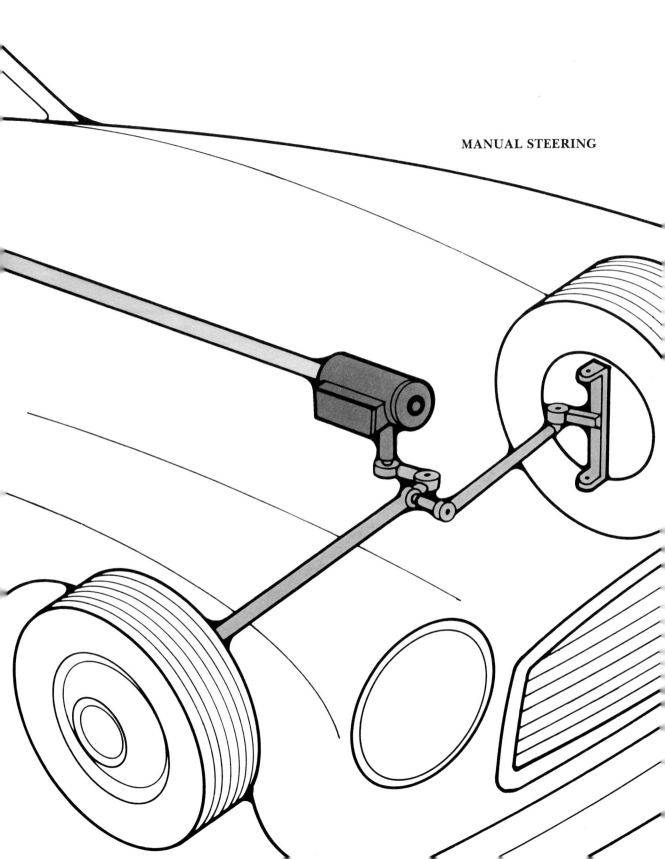

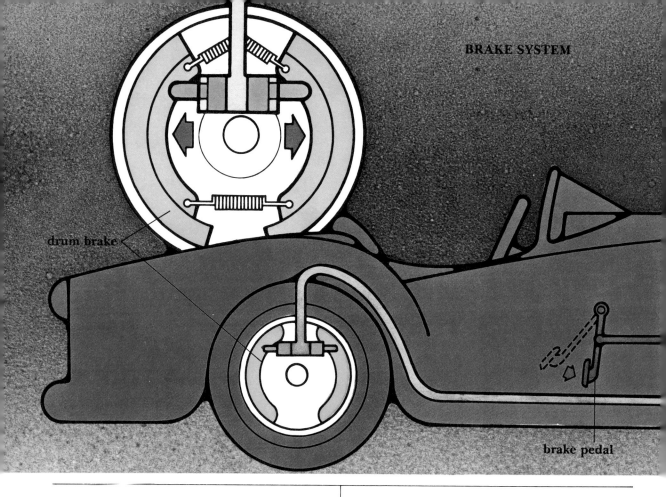

drum brake

brake pedal

Another system is the brake system. This slows the car down or makes it stop. You often find two kinds of brakes on a car. One is the disc brake. The other is the drum brake.

The disc brake is used on the front wheels. A drum brake works on the rear wheels.

A disc brake is a round piece of metal. It is found on the inside of a wheel. It moves with the wheel. A clamp fits around the top of the disc. The clamp holds pads that can move against the disc.

When we press on the brake pedal, we send fluid to the disc brake. This fluid causes the clamp to press against the brake pads. These, in turn, press against the disc. This slows the wheel down or keeps it from turning.

disc brake

The working parts of a drum brake are inside a piece of metal shaped like a drum. This is found next to a wheel. It also moves with the wheel.

Inside the drum are two curved pieces of metal. These are brake shoes. One side of the shoes is covered with rough material, just like the disc of a friction clutch. The pressure of your foot on the brake pedal is sent to the brake shoes. They press against the drum. When this happens, the wheel slows or stops moving.

As you take your foot off the brake pedal, springs in the brake move the shoes away from the drum. The wheel now turns again.

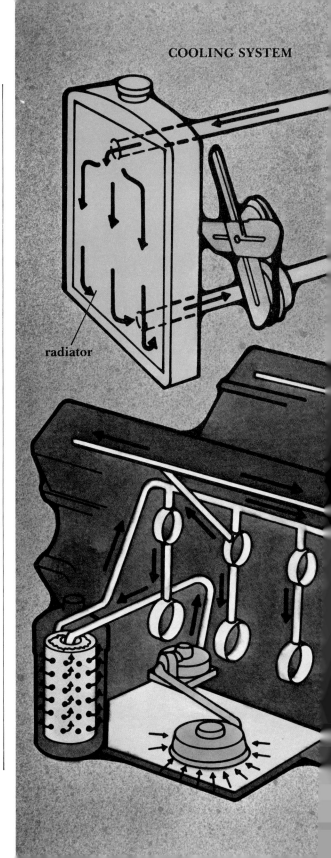

radiator

The electrical system is the next one we look at.

As we said, when the motor is running, the generator produces electricity. And our car needs about 1,000 feet (310 meters) of wire to carry that power to where it is needed. You might be surprised at how many places there are.

We mentioned the battery, the distributor, and the spark plugs before. But a car's headlights and taillights need electricity too. And so do the radio, air conditioner, and horn. So do the fuel gauge, lights on the instrument panel, and the windshield wipers.

The lights inside the car use electricity. So does the heater that keeps you warm during cold weather.

A car has other systems that help it to run well. The oil system takes oil from a pan under the engine, through the engine's moving parts, and back again. Oil helps the pistons to go up and down smoothly. It helps the crankshaft to turn without getting worn out.

Oil helps cool the engine. So does water. A car carries water in the radiator in front of the engine.

A small pump draws water from the bottom of the radiator. It sends the water through passages around the cylinders. This is where most of the heat is.

As water takes heat from the engine, it flows through other tubes back to the radiator. There, as air blows on it, the water loses much of the heat. It then goes to the pump and around the engine again. Like oil, water moves around all the time the engine is running.

LUBRICATION (OIL) SYSTEM

Finally, we come to what is called the suspension system. Suspension here means "to hold away from." A car's suspension system holds the body away from bumps in the road.

Each wheel on a car has its own suspension system. Springs make up one part of it. What are called shock absorbers make up the other part. Springs and shock absorbers are found on the front and rear axles next to the wheels.

A shock absorber is a long cylinder with a piston in it. When a wheel hits a bump, the spring takes up some of the force. At the same time, the piston in the shock absorber moves upward. This takes in, or absorbs, some of the bump's force too. The shock and the springs cut down on the up and down motion a bump causes.

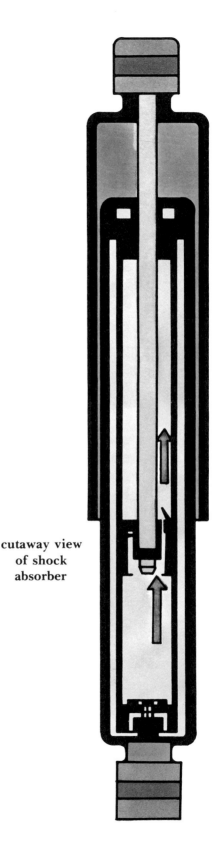

cutaway view
of shock
absorber

springs

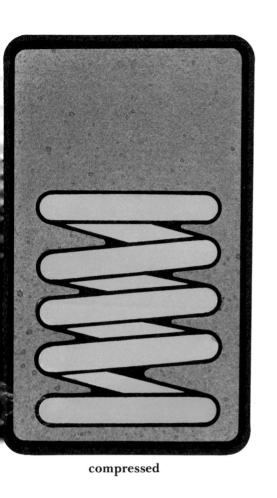

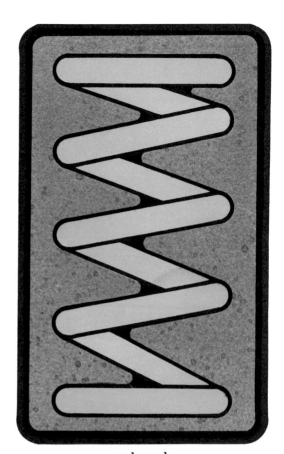

compressed

released

shock absorbers

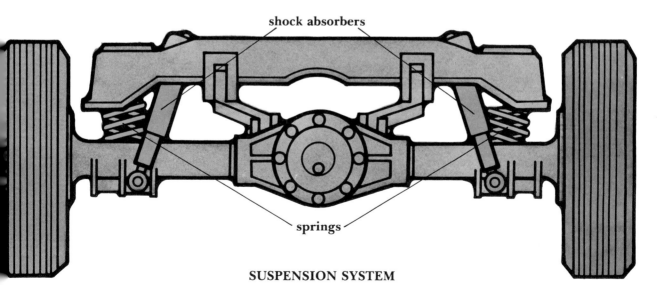

springs

SUSPENSION SYSTEM

SPECIAL CARS

Now let's look at a few of the many kinds of cars in the world.

Some cars have 4-wheel drive. Here, both front and rear wheels get power from the engine. This helps the car climb steep hills. And it can travel over land where there are no roads. One 4-wheel drive was built for the army. It was called a "General Purpose" car. From the letters G.P. came the word jeep. Dune buggies are also 4-wheel drives.

Some cars have electric motors. The motor gets power from batteries. This car must stop now and then to have its batteries recharged. Some people think there should be more electric cars. They are quiet. They don't pollute the air. Most of all, they don't use expensive gasoline.

Racers are another kind of car, and there are many of them. Some have huge rear wheels. These give the racer lots of push. The front wheels are thin. They look like bicycle wheels. Some of these racers don't have brakes. The driver lets out a parachute that fills with air to stop the racer.

Some racing cars are called midgets. They are very small, with tiny seats. The driver has to take a deep breath to squeeze into one.

One large and special racing car was called the *Spirit of America*. It looked like an airplane without wings. A jet engine, as on an airplane, made it go. The *Spirit of America* once traveled at more than 600 miles (965 kilometers) per hour.

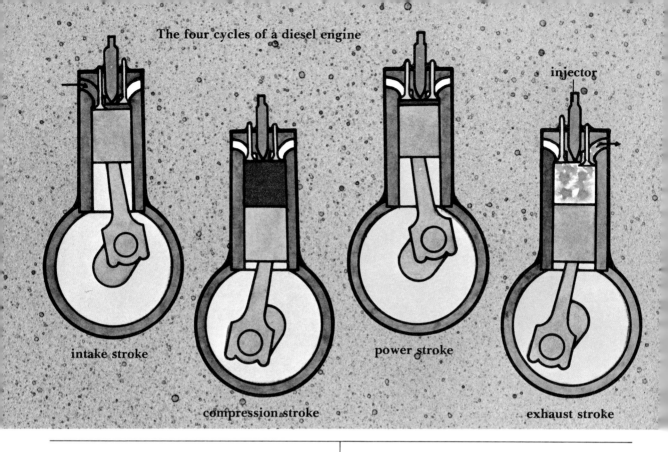

The four cycles of a diesel engine

intake stroke

compression stroke

power stroke

injector

exhaust stroke

There are also different kinds of engines. One is the diesel. It runs on oil instead of gasoline. The diesel has no spark plugs. Fuel and air are squeezed tightly together to make the mixture explode. This drives the cylinders. Three cars with diesel engines are the Volkswagon Rabbit, Mercedes, and Oldsmobile. Large trucks also have diesel engines.

Still another kind of engine is the Wankel. It has no cylinders

diesel car

44

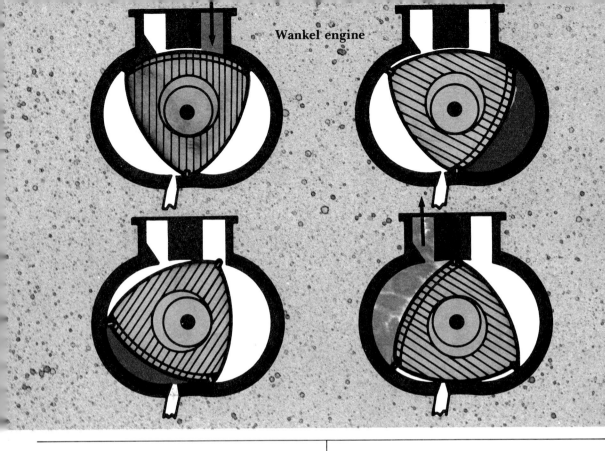

Wankel engine

car with rotary engine

at all. Instead, it has rotors. Rotors turn like wheels. When their power is connected to the driveshaft, power goes to the rear wheels to make the car go. Car builders are still just trying out the Wankel engine.

There are many, many more kinds of cars than we can talk about here. And in the future there might be others. The car you will drive might be very different from the ones you see today.

45

PRONUNCIATION GUIDE

These symbols have the same sound as the darker letters in the sample words.

ə	balloon, ago
a	map, have
ä	father, car
b	ball, rib
d	did, add
e	bell, get
f	fan, soft
g	good, big
h	hurt, ahead
i	rip, ill
ī	side, sky
j	join, germ
k	king, ask
l	let, cool
m	man, same
n	no, turn
ō	cone, know
ȯ	all, saw
p	part, scrap
r	root, tire
s	so, press
sh	shoot, machine
t	to, stand
ü	pool, lose
u̇	put, book
v	view, give
w	wood, glowing
y	yes, year
′	strong accent
′	weak accent

GLOSSARY

These words are defined the way they are used in the book.

accelerator (ik sel′ ə rat′ ər) a flat pedal on the floor of a car that, when pressed, causes more fuel to flow through the engine and thus causes the car to speed up

axle (ak′ səl) a shaft or a rod around which a pair of wheels turns

battery (bat′ a rē) a square object in a car's engine in which electricity is made

brake (brāk) a device that presses against a wheel to slow or stop its movement

carburetor (kär′ bə rāt′ ər) a device in a car's engine that mixes gasoline and air together

clutch (kləch) part of a car's transmission that connects and disconnects gears

countershaft (kau̇nt′ ər shaft′) a rod that is connected by gears to the transmission shaft and the output shaft, and helps send the engine's movements to the wheels

crankshaft (krangk′ shaft′) a crooked piece of metal at the bottom of the engine which turns to move the pistons up and down

cylinder (sil′ ən dər) a rounded

container in an engine which holds a piston and a gasoline and air mixture when the car is running

distributor (dis trib′ yət ər) a device in an engine that sends electricity to the spark plugs in the proper order

engine (en′ jən) the machine in a car that changes fuel into the force and movement that drives the car

exhaust (ig zȯst′) the used gas that is released from a car engine into the air

gasoline (gas′ ə lēn′) a liquid fuel that catches fire easily and is used in car engines

gearshift (gir′ shift′) a device connected to the transmission of a car that connects and disconnects the gears

generator (jen′ ə rāt′ ər) a motor in a car's engine that makes electricity

ignition (ig nish′ ən) the device that, at the turn of a key, sends electricity to the battery in order to start a car

output shaft (aut′ put′ shaft) a long rod that carries movement from the crankshaft in the engine to the rear wheels

piston (pis′ tən) a device shaped like a tin can that moves up and down in a cylinder to squeeze and release the gasoline-air mixture

power-train system (paur′ trān sis′ təm) the system of shafts and gears that sends the power of the engine to the rear axle

radiator (rād′ ē āt′ ər) a device in the front of an engine that holds and cools the water

shock absorber (shäk′ əb sörb′ er) a device connected to a car's wheel that takes up, or absorbs, the force of bumps in a road

spark plug (spärk′ pləg′) a part that fits into the top of a cylinder, and makes a spark that causes the fuel in the cylinder to explode

suspension (sə spen′ chən) the system made up of springs and shock absorbers that holds and protects a car from bumps and jolts

transmission (trans mish′ ən) the entire system of shafts and gears that sends power from driver to the engine to the wheels

transmission shaft (trans mish′ ən shaft′) the rod that sends power from the clutch to the countershaft

INDEX